35 BEST WORK FROM HOME JOBS

Best Remote Jobs, Earn money Both online and offline, Passive Income, Financial Freedom and Finding the right Home jobs.

BHARLINE BINNY

Copyright 2021 Morgan.

This book is subject to copyright policy. All rights are reserved, whether the entire or component of the material, particularly the rights of transformation, reprinting, recycling illustration, broadcasting, duplicating on microfilm, or in any other way. No part or even the whole of this book or contents may be produced or even transmitted or reproduced in any way, be it electronic or paper form or by any means, electronic or mechanical, also include recording or by any information storage or retrieval system, without prior written permission the copyright, **Morgan L**

TABLE OF CONTENTS

INTRODUCTION 4
PART 1: STARTING A WORK FROM HOME BUSINESS 6
HOME BASED JOBS 7
ADVANTAGES AND DISADVANTAGES 8
PART 2: WORK FROM HOME JOBS 10
BUY PRODUCTS AND SELL THEM ONLINE 13
COPYWRITING, PROOFREADING, FREELANCE WRITING, AND EDITING JOBS: 14
PRINT ON DEMAND JOB: 16
ONLINE TEACHING JOBS 17
DATA ENTRY JOBS 19
AFFILIATING MARKETING JOBS: 22
SELL YOUR SERVICE OR EXPERTISE: 23
BLOGGING HOME JOB: 24
WRITING REVIEW JOB: 25
CONTENT CREATOR JOB: 26
SOCIAL MEDIA MANAGER OR MODERATOR: 27
REAL ESTATE AND TRAVELLING AGENTS: 28
CALL AGENT JOB: 29
BUY AN EXISTING E-COMMENCE 30

CHECK OR MYSTERY SHOPPER JOB: 32
FIVERR ONLINE JOBS: 33
FITNESS CENTER COUCHING: 34
PROFESSIONAL HEALTH CODER: 35
AUTHOR- AMAZON KDP JOB: 37
SMARTPHONE APP AND OTHER JOBS: 38
SEARCH ENGINE EVALUATORS: 39
CONSULTANCY JOBS: 40
MAIL ORDER BUSINESS: 41
SELLING PHOTOS AND IMAGES: 42
PAID EXPERT OR PROFESSIONAL JOB: 43
VIRTUAL ASSISTANCE JOBS: 44
POLL TAKER AND SURVEY E-COUNT: 45
HOME MASSAGE SERVICE: 47
CHAT AND EMAIL SUPPORT SERVICE: 48
YOUTUBE CHANNEL: 49

INTRODUCTION

We live in a great and wonderful time where you can earn a living as well as get an accredited college degree from the comfort of your own home. Finding a job that you can do from home would give you a lot of freedom and it comes with a lot of flexibility. So if you are up for it, we have compiled a list of the best "work from home jobs".

Last year, the COVID-19 pandemic impacted negatively on the job market in the United States. More than 30 million Americans applied for unemployment benefits for the first time in the months since the pandemic was proclaimed a national emergency, as well as the unemployment rate, reached double digits.

Working from home jobs has long been a desirable choice for younger and older people. The positive news is that you will now find a variety of work-from-home opportunities in a variety of fields and at various levels of expertise.

PART 1: STARTING A WORK FROM HOME BUSINESS

You might imagine starting a commercial real estate, commuting to an office, or managing employees when you consider owning and running a firm. However, as home businesses become more common, more people are finding ways to use workplace flexibility to explore entrepreneurship from the comfort of their own homes.

Home-based businesses take many forms in today's wired society, where technology allows us greater choice in how and where we live.

Some of them need you to transform a spare room into a product store, while others can be managed entirely online. However, you will usually launch these types of companies using the little space you have at home and resources you already have.

HOME BASED JOBS

A home-based job is a business that you can set up as well as run from the comfort of your own home, whether it's full-time or part-time. Some home-based jobs, especially those that sell online and just don't buy as well as store a lot of inventory, can also be run on the go, so you don't have to be confined to your home.

ADVANTAGES AND DISADVANTAGES

Naturally, there are advantages and disadvantages to weigh when considering whether or not to start a home-based job.

ADVANTAGES:

- It is easy to start on like the physical businesses that go through a lot of registrations.
- You have a wide range of customers both local and international.
- It has a fewer overhead cost.
- it can solely be done by one person.
- Enjoy the comfort of your home.
- It has a flexible work time and life balance.
- No or Less capital to start.

DISADVANTAGES:

- You may enjoy some level of freedom but there is also a soon level of loneliness attached to a home-based job.
- Your business may outgrow your capacity at some point in time which will require you to hire an employee.

- Less teamwork, Brainstorming, and sharing ideas may not be available in home-based jobs.
- It can be so discouraging mostly if you are not making money.

PART 2: WORK FROM HOME JOBS

I have some years of professional experience from home in a variety of jobs as well as have made a living doing so. This is a way of life that I genuinely enjoy.

There are many work-from-home options available in a variety of industries. It's easier to make an educated decision about your future position when you consider your skills, experience, and enthusiasm.

Working from home is the perfect choice because it allows you to set your convenient time that you will like to work and also work from the convenience of your own home, as well as spend time with your family. There are several works from home jobs that pay well and allow you to work part-time and full-time.

I'll show you the best work-at-home jobs that pay $20-$70 or even more than an hour or more. I have even conducted extensive studies on other work-at-home opportunities.

The following are 30 remote jobs for anyone who feels like working from his comfort home.

BUY PRODUCTS AND SELL THEM ONLINE

You can buy products in large quantities and sell them online. Firstly, you need to make sure that such products are selling. What you need to do is just to have a landing page and also advertise your products on social media like Facebook, Google, and Instagram.

COPYWRITING, PROOFREADING, FREELANCE WRITING, AND EDITING JOBS:

A freelance writer is an opportunity that has exploded on the internet world. Anybody can work as freelance writers from the comfort of their own homes and make enough money.

To get hired, what you need to do is post any examples of your writing to freelance portals like Upwork or Freelancer.com. There are a lot of possibilities if you can write without making grammatical errors.

However, the sum of money you make can be determined by the content of your writing as well as the blog or individual you are writing for.

The following are freelance writing options that you can venture into:

1	Web content writing	Editing and proofreading
2	Copywriting	Newspaper and article writing
3	Technical and social writing	Business writing
4	Social writing	Educational and Academic writing

You can charge based on per word which is between $0.05 to 2$ depend on what you want to charge.

PRINT ON DEMAND JOB:

A print-on-demand service, like dropshipping business, doesn't allow you to keep inventory or ship it yourself. Print-on-demand also allows you to personalize white-label merchandise with your exclusive designs.

Books, t-shirts, jackets, backpacks, blankets, pillows, mugs, sneakers, hoodies, phone covers, watches, and more are among the items you can market, depending on the retailer you want to deal with.

Many print-on-demand companies cater to a small market or, better still, a common identity.

ONLINE TEACHING JOBS

Online teaching is also another great way for college students, stay-at-home mothers, and freelancers to supplement their income. With online teaching jobs, you can comfortably receive $1000-$4500 a month if you work only 2-6 hours per day. You should choose a subject that interests you and hold a one-hour video call session on it.

Google Classroom:
You can make use of Google classroom for your learning device. The google classroom is absolutely free service available for colleges, instructors, teachers, and students, also for individuals with a Google account. It's easy for students and teachers in the classroom.

Some subjects you can teach are: Mathematics, social science, legal and law, literature, English language, accounting and finance, economics, physics and chemistry, and a lot more.

You can charge as low as $5-10 per hour. Some of the sites you can join are chegg..com. tutors..com, brainfuse, and Pearson.

DATA ENTRY JOBS

I do hear some people say that; there are no legitimate or suitable data entry jobs available online. This is not true because they are a lot and in fact, I will provide some websites for data entry jobs, I will provide you with a list of data entry online firm that offer different types of work.

The second fallacy is that data entry positions do not pay well enough. This is untrue, according to Statistics, data entry jobs earned between $15,000 and $50,000 a year in 2021.

The followings are some of the data entry jobs:

- Excel data entry jobs.
- Formatting some files in Microsoft Word or Microsoft excel.
- Converting image files
- Converting client's data.
- Inputting inventory data entry.
- A lot more.

Some websites for data entry jobs are:
- Upwork..com
- Freelancing

- Data plus
- Konsus
- Cassinfo

AFFILIATING MARKETING JOBS:

I'm sure you have heard of affiliate marketing before and so, working mostly at home is always one of the easiest ways to make a lot of money. You become an associate partner of a merchant or network in affiliate marketing. You market the merchant's goods and are compensated when necessary action is taken via your marketing, you will be compensated for each sale and it is free signup on the website.

Affiliate marketing can be done in a variety of ways. Blogging has shown to be one of the most successful methods. Other options include PPC advertising, social media websites mostly like Facebook and Instagram, and email marketing, among others. A successful affiliate marketer will receive upwards of $1000-$10,000 per month. You would learn a lot about affiliate marketing to have a good understanding of it.

SELL YOUR SERVICE OR EXPERTISE:

Starting to sell services at home is much easier than starting to sell goods, but the difficulty is allocating your little time. Once it comes to running a service-based enterprise, the adage "time is money" is never more accurate.

Designers and marketers, for example, can freelance or work for other firms while juggling several customers, often from the comfort of their own homes. Others can work based on appointments and bookings, providing services to individuals on a one-on-one basis.

BLOGGING HOME JOB:

Blogging is among the most common work from home jobs right now. Regardless of age group, whether Generation X or Millennial, both of these demographics enjoy blogging.

Writing about your favorite topics is what blogging is all about. All have a love for something or is a specialist in it. You can use your blog to share your experiences, insights, and tips.

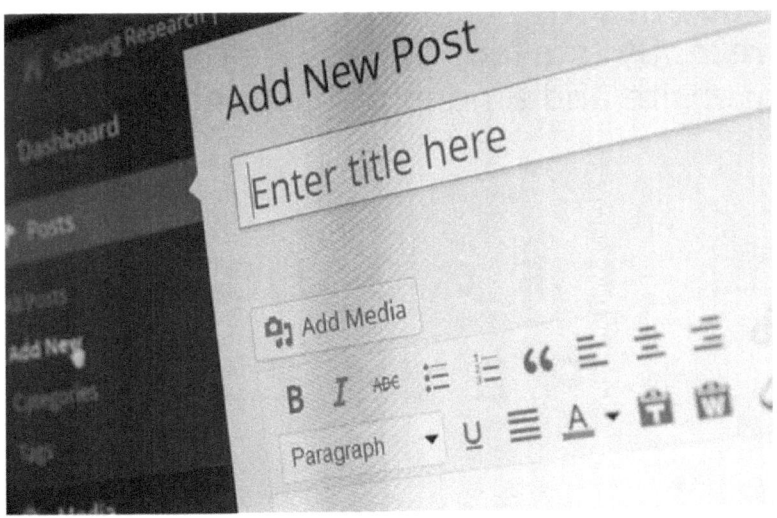

Today, beginning a blog is incredibly easy. A ten-year-old child will start a blog. You can begin a free blog, but if you have a small budget (less than $75). In comparison to a free blog, a self-hosted WordPress blog is the highest. You can start a blog for as low as $50-$200.

WRITING REVIEW JOB:

Writing reviews is a full-time or even a part-time job that can be done from home in your comfort zone. You write a review for a movie, a new restaurant you recently visited, a hotel/resort you recently stayed at, as well as a new website and among other things.

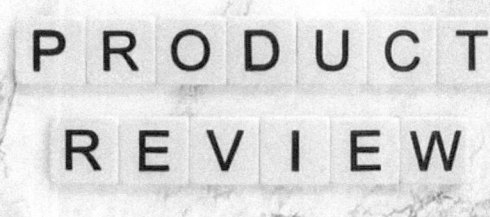

You will compose reviews for several different blogs, online magazines, newsletters, and other online publications. You can work separately from home and send your completed work via email.

You can earn as much as $2000-$40,000.

CONTENT CREATOR JOB:

If you are a content creator with a large online audience, or if you have always wanted to create your forum, YouTube channel as well as Instagram account, or podcast, some of the previous ideas on this list will help you expand and monetize your audience.

You may also consider being an affiliate, which involves selling other people's goods or services in exchange for a fee or commission or taking payment for supported content, which allows advertisers to connect with your audience.

SOCIAL MEDIA MANAGER OR MODERATOR:

Social media coordinators and moderators are in control of many internet forums including social media sites. Your work entails assisting users, responding to their comments and suggestions, deleting offensive comments, managing discussion posts, and so on. Working from home as a social media coordinator or moderator will pay $10 – $30 per hour.

REAL ESTATE AND TRAVELLING AGENTS:

If you live in a metropolitan area, this is a very lucrative venture. People who have access will work as Real Estate Agents as well as broker transactions. You collect commission from both the seller as well as the buyer while you work as an agent. You can start this business from home.

CALL AGENT JOB:

Customer Support Agents will also serve consumers from the convenience of their own homes, rather than sitting in a workplace. Companies used to outsource or subcontract customer support service to other countries, but now they contract with people such as you and me right here in the United States.

This is a burgeoning market with a bright future ahead of it. For picking and answering calls, you will need a device, special apps, and other tools.

Rather than being charged by the hour, you are paid by the minute. Call center agents that work from home receive between $30,000 and $36,000 a year on average.

BUY AN EXISTING E-COMMENCE

Consider purchasing an already made e-commerce platform if you're more interested in merely investing in a stream of income that you can manage from the comfort of your home or even on the go.

Prices can differ significantly depending on several variables, including overall sales produced, benefit opportunity, available assets (such as an email list), inventory, and so on. Some sellers will also take you under their wing and show you how to run their company.

Exchange is a Shopify-powered marketplace for purchasing and selling e-commerce platforms. You can search the listings for companies that suit your budget, skill level, and requirements.

CHECK OR MYSTERY SHOPPER JOB:

Big firms and businesses rely on you to find out what customers think of their goods and services, which are available in a variety of locations around the globe.

They employ Mystery shoppers to gather feedback on people's shopping experiences. As a mystery or check shopper, you would be required to complete tasks such as eating in a restaurant, purchasing items, testing a program, driving a car, and so on.

Being a gifted writer is a valuable talent to have if you desire to work as a mystery shopper.

In just five to ten minutes, you can make $5 of $10 by mystery shopping online. You will raise $22 to $180 offline, but it will take 3 to 6 hours.

FIVERR ONLINE JOBS:

I don't feel I have to explain Fiverr to you. It's the safest means to go if you are hunting for a micro-job as a freelancer. Micro Jobs are small pieces of work such as logo design, code fixes, article writing, animation as well as video production, marketing, and so forth.

Every 5 seconds, a gig is purchased on Fiverr. According to your information, over 40 million projects were completed to date. You can make from $50 to $19,000 in Fiverr. You sign up right now and begin providing your services.

FITNESS CENTER COUCHING:

If you are unable to teach online, you can do so offline by opening a coaching center as well as a mini-gym coach in your house. You could start by gathering children from your community and educating them in groups. A batch of ten students is sufficient; you can teach two or three batches per day. You should grow until you have established yourself.

To open a coaching center, you don't need much money. However, you must publicize your coaching center in your community.

PROFESSIONAL HEALTH CODER:

The work of a medical or health coder is somewhat close to that of a medical transcriptionist, with one minor exception. Health coders get their input by reading patient records, while transcriptionists listen to doctors or their audio/videotape and afterward type down codes depending on that.

Health coders would read patient charts and determine the patient's medical background, including diagnoses and medications previously administered.

A health coder can create medical codes based on records and notes to transcribe a patient's experience into a "shorthand" style of writing that health care professionals and insurance firms may understand.

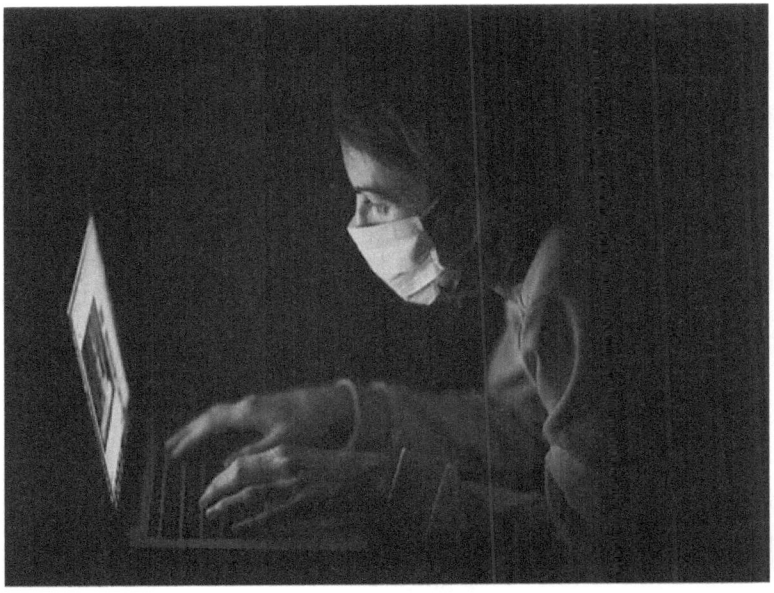

Health coders earn up to 20$ per hour and $20,000-$80,000 annually.

AUTHOR- AMAZON KDP JOB:

Authors will use KDP Publishing to self-publish eBooks including paperback books. All you have to do is upload your book files for eBooks, which will show in the Kindle store immediately after review from kdp amazon team as an eBook that users can order and buy immediately.

You don't have to pay for the printing of the book; instead, you get paid a royalty when it sells. You have the price as well as the royalty. Immediately after upload your ebook or paperback, Amazon tells you how much it would cost — $2.50-$40 for a 200-page book depend on printing options lick black, color, or creamy, for example, you make up to $1.50 to $100 per book you sell.

SMARTPHONE APP AND OTHER JOBS:

Your mobile phone can be used to earn money. There are a plethora of money-making applications available that can help you make money while having fun.

All you need or require to do is download these applications to your smartphone and complete a few basic tasks. Depending on the software you select, you are rewarded when you finish a mission.

Here are some of the apps rewardable, checkpoint, gigwalk, and Shopkick.

SEARCH ENGINE EVALUATORS:

Search engines such as Google, Bing, and Yahoo change daily. Each corporation is up against stiff competition from its peers. As a result, to remain ahead of the competition, they aim to have the best search results for their customers.

As a result, once their search algorithms are updated, they request you to run searches on a list of keywords. In exchange, you have input on the search result's content accurately.

CONSULTANCY JOBS:

Education, business, profession, human capital, real estate, accounting, and other fields of expertise will help you become a successful consultant. You may consult from the comfort of your own home using Skype. You charge a fee for each appointment or session.

MAIL ORDER BUSINESS:

Another perfect way to work from home and make money offline is through a mail-order company or direct mail marketing. You send out a mass mailing to advertise goods or services, and the customer places an order by mail.

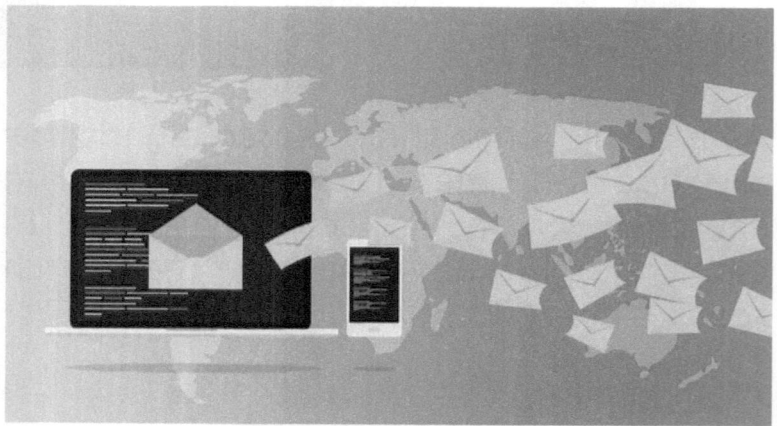

As an upfront outlay, all you will need are some envelopes, stamps, as well as other stationery items, as well as printing fees.

SELLING PHOTOS AND IMAGES:

You can make much more money using your mobile and You can use your smartphone to take quality photos and sell them on sites like Shutterstock, Fotolia, as well as iStock Photo.

You don't even need to purchase a camera because most smartphones come with built-in advanced cameras.

PAID EXPERT OR PROFESSIONAL JOB:

Make money by providing professional advice to people online on a variety of topics.

Before you can give people professional advice, you must first master your field. You may offer advice on different subject matters, including businesses, vehicles, fitness, pets, legal and law, job, technology, and so on.

If your recommendation is well-received, the firm will compensate you for your services. You can easily earn $600 – $10,000 per month by working 2 to 8 hours per day.

VIRTUAL ASSISTANCE JOBS:

Virtual assistance is one of the best jobs you can do at home and make money.

Jobs as a virtual assistant are actually in high demand. As a virtual assistant, you can help administrators and executives with activities such as bookkeeping, filing, answering calls, handling schedules, writing posts, and so on. You will even be asked to do one-off jobs from time to time.

You will need outstanding listening skills, excellent writing skills, and a thorough understanding of Microsoft Word and Excel, Google Apps, Dropbox, and other similar programs.

This job can be completed from home (online work from home) and pays between $5 and $70 per hour. You can visit the Upwork website to register.

POLL TAKER AND SURVEY E-COUNT:

A poll taker's job is somewhat close to a survey taker's job. You will perform polls on different subject matter, including politics, philosophy, sports, and consumer products.

During the voting or election season, for example, the majority of the questions would be about politics.

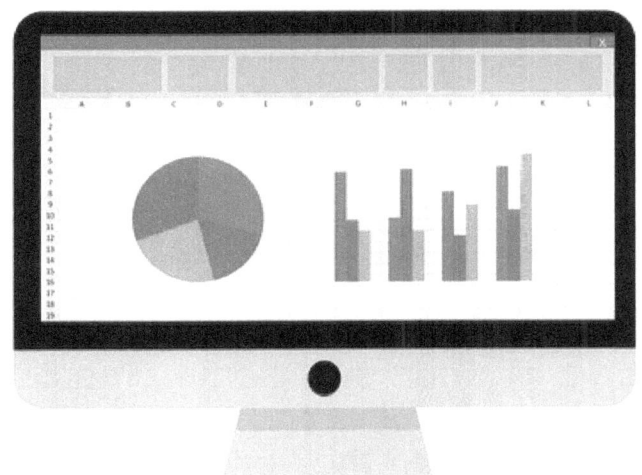

Depending on the duration of the poll, you would only have to answer 3 to 16 basic questions. Polls are simple to complete and only require a basic understanding of English.

It's a very versatile job that you love to do at any time of day. What you need is an Internet-connected device. The length of a sample determines how much you get paying. Taking a poll usually pays anywhere from $1 to $45.

You can visit the following website:
- Branded surveys.
- Toluna
- Inbox pounds
- One poll
- Life points
- Swagbucks

HOME MASSAGE SERVICE:

You provide massage services from the comfort of your own home. People will come to your doorsteps after seeing the advertisement in the newspaper.

You can run a new spa or parlor in your home with minimal investment if you are a qualified and experienced masseuse or masseur.

You will make a good sum of money.

CHAT AND EMAIL SUPPORT SERVICE:

Companies wouldn't want to leave every stone unexplored when it usually comes to customer service.

Apart from traditional channels such as phone calls, nearly every big organization now uses online chat to communicate with their clients.

Most of these chat service agents operate from home. Agents who can connect by email are also employed.

You can earn 10-15 per hour. Annually between $7000-$14,000.

YOUTUBE CHANNEL:

You can begin a YouTube channel from the comfort of your own home. YouTube is the largest video-viewing website on the internet, so I am sure you have heard of it.

You can earn money by beginning your own precious YouTube channel as well as marketing your own or other companies services and products, or you can join the YouTube Partner Program.

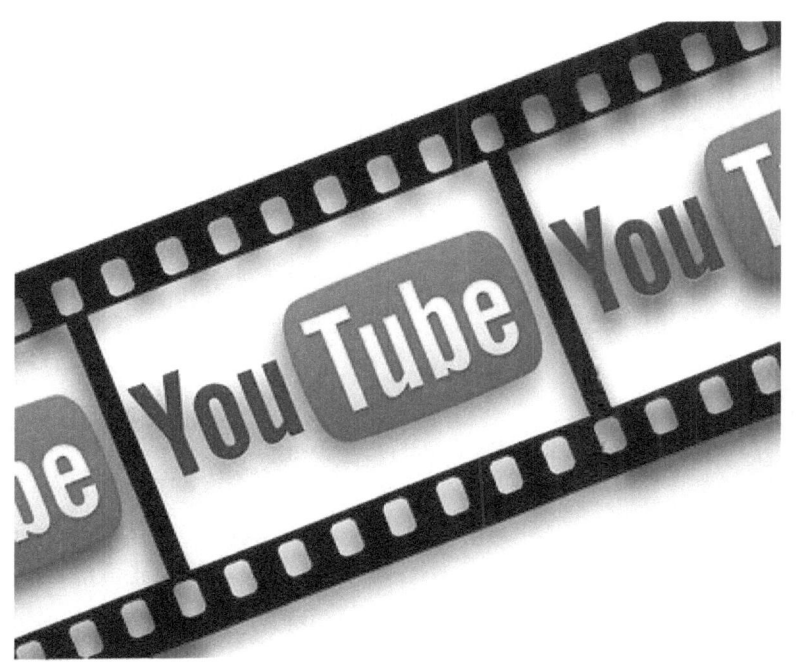

HOW TO START:

In terms of setup, YouTube is similar to every other social networking channel. However, the following are the steps you need to take for you to build a video channel that can attract hundreds, thousands, or perhaps even millions of regular viewers:

Step 1: Create your youtube channel.
Step 2: Post videos.
Step 3: Build your audience.

Step 4: Cross promote your videos.
Step 5: Set up a youtube account to monetize with ads.
Step 6: Monetize your youtube channels with affiliating marketing.
Step 7: Check your stat and use the information wisely.
Step 8: Apply for a youtube partnership.

www.ingramcontent.com/pod-product-compliance
Lightning Source LLC
Chambersburg PA
CBHW030513220526
45464CB00006B/2770